717 4SP

FRESH VOICES

An anthology of poetry and prose written by children and young people and offering resource material for Christian education and worship

Compiled by Donald Hilton

NATIONAL CHRISTIAN EDUCATION COUNCIL

Robert Denholm House
Nutfield, Redhill, Surrey, RH1 4HW

To Jeremy and Christopher
and the many other children and
young people who have been my
teachers

Other books by Donald Hilton:

Boy into Man
Girl into Woman
Words to Share
Questions Jesus Wouldn't Answer...?

Prayers for the Church Community
(in collaboration with Roy Chapman)

In instances where copyright, or the material itself, requires it, spellings and punctuation have
been retained in their original form.

First published in 1979
Collection © Donald H. Hilton

0 7197 0219 4

Typeset by Surrey Graphics Ltd, Dorking, Surrey
Printed and bound by Page Bros (Norwich) Ltd, Norwich, Norfolk

CONTENTS

INTRODUCTION

This anthology is an invitation to listen to children and young people. The contributors range in age from five to twenty years. Whatever their age they have a valid experience of life on which to call as they express themselves through poetry and prose. We must be as carefully critical of the work of children and young people as we are of that written by anyone else but we shall miss a great deal unless we develop the ability simply to listen to their voices.

FRESH VOICES has several aims. First, it provides the opportunity to share the experience and insights of children and young people. Secondly, since it includes many previously unpublished items it preserves material which might otherwise have been lost in staffroom cupboards, church rooms and neglected piles of school magazines. Thirdly, since the material is categorised in themes it offers resources which will be useful in religious education in day schools, and in Christian education and worship in churches.

Some of the items clearly arise from specific incidents in the lives of the young people eg, see items 53, 60, 62, 69 and especially 31. Others have arisen from the young people's ability to reflect on their experience and see its wider significance eg, see 30, 45, 78 and 109. The imaginative insight, which is often lost as we grow older, is seen in much of the work as also is the ability to step into the experience of other people and feel their joy or pain. A number of items are overtly religious and will be readily useful in worship and religious education but they have all been selected for the way in which they probe basic human responses and emotions and so illustrate man's search for his own identity, his relationships with other people and his response to his total environment thus providing clues for our spiritual pilgrimage. The index has been arranged with this in mind.

Without doubt a good deal more material is available which could extend this anthology. The compiler would always be glad to receive examples of young people's work against the possibility of further publications. This book would not have been possible without the co-operation of many young people, their teachers, schools and friends.

Donald Hilton

Thank you

1

A psalm of praise

Praise the Lord all flowers and trees,
Sing his praises wasps and bees.

Daffodils and small primroses,
Show your thanks in groups and poses.

Skip and hop you baby rabbit,
Make his praise your daily habit.

Worship him you clouds and fogs,
Wag your tails you happy dogs.

Dig for joy all moles and worms,
And worship him in happy terms.

Come forth from your cosy lair,
And join the throng, O little bear.

Praise the Lord, O night and day,
The moon's pale light and sun's bright ray.

Shout his praises, old and young,
Keep thanks and praises on your tongue.

Lift up your voices large and small;
Sing praise to him who made us all.

Mary Wakelin, 10 years

2

Noise

I like noise:
The whispering of branches.
The weeping of willows.
The flap of our bedclothes.
The thud of our pillows.
The thumping of engines.
The screeching of brakes.
The noises of people
Who sit munching cakes.
The crashing of dustbins.
The singing of songs.
The jingle of teabells
And loud dinner gongs.
The turning of pages.
The rattle of pens.
The screeching and squawking
Of roosters and hens.
The howl of the north wind.
The beat of the rain.
The incessant turn
Of the black weather vane.
The thumping of footsteps.
The clicking of heels.
The noises that cards make
When somebody deals.
The lapping of oceans.
The gurgling of streams.
The noise of supporters
Who yell for their teams.
The creaking our house makes
When everything's dark.
And the rusty complaints
From the swings in the park.
The jingle of money
In shopkeepers' tills.
And the rustle from cheque books
As folk pay their bills.
The screams from the girls
And the yells of the boys.
The laughter of children
Who play with their toys.
— I like noise.

Rachael Chaldecott, 14 years

3

Thank you, Jesus

Dear Lord,
I say this prayer to thank you
For all the beautiful things you have given us,
Like the sun that makes everything look clean and bright;
For the snow which brings along the little robin,
The mountains and the green trees, the rivers and the sea.
I know you give us this free
So that rich and poor we can all enjoy them, and we do.
Thank you, Lord. Amen

Gillian Ingram, 7 years

4

Taste

Fresh baked bread, newly from the oven,
Rich plum pudding, fat and round,
Hot buttered crumpets, smooth dark chocolate,
Warm baked potatoes, oven browned.

Ice cream sodas, cold and creamy,
Sponge treacle puddings, fluffy and light,
Large juicy melons sprinkled with sugar,
Hot yellow pancakes, tossed just right.

Hot roasted chestnuts, straight from the embers,
Freshly made coffee, fragrant and strong,
Thick lentil soup poured from the saucepan,
Crisp sausage rolls, round, thin and long.

Round cream doughnuts, jammy and gooey,
Beef stew with dumplings tasty and thick,
Soft currant bread, spread thickly with butter,
Ripe crunchy apples, just take your pick.

All of these are my favourite eatables,
Sticky, stodgy, like glue or like paste,
Some of them crispy, gooey and fluffy,
Because all of this poem is all about taste.

Vanessa Lincoln, 12 years

5

The long day has worn out my body.
I give thanks
that I was able to work hard
for a good cause —
and that I earned some money.

Thanks,
Lord,
that I could use my voice,
my shoulders,
my arms,
my hands.

Lord,
I am tired,
I am falling asleep,
Hallelujah for this day!

A young Ghanaian

6

Waking up

Heavy eyes,
gentle breathing,
Peace
complete,
yet,
desire for activity
so strong
it recreates;
combining with
Happiness and
Thankfulness
so intense
they hurt;
compelling me to ask:
Why me?
Why such joy for me?
Reflected in the
grey light
and the rejoicing
song of birds,
communicating
a sense of meaning,

Purpose
so profound
I hold my breath,
momentarily
frightened
lest the moment
pass
leaving only
guilt
that I should have
so much,
when all around
Despair,
Apathy,
Hopelessness
and Cynicism,
govern
the hearts and minds
of individuals
with infinite
Potential
to experience
the Joy
which overwhelms me.

Mary Wakelin, 18 years

Who am I?

7

Me

What am I?
  A boy.

Why am I?
I can never arrive
At a satisfactory
  Answer
As to why
  I am.
But there must be a reason,
For without a reason,
What is the point of
  Me
Being around to eat
  Good food
And using up
Useful space?

So,
Why
Am I?

Anon

8

Before being born

When I am born
Let my eyes twinkle like diamonds bright
And the dew-shine on the grass.
Let flowers grow where I tread.
May the sky shine blue as blue as it has ever been.
When I am born.

Helen Lewis, 10 years

9

If I was a caterpillar

If I was a caterpillar
What would I do?
Would I live on my own
Would I know what to do
Would I know if I saw you
When I was first born
Would I know where to go
if I sat on a lawn
Would I know if I changed
Would I know if I could
Would I know where I lived
Would I know where I stood
Would I change to a moth
Would I hide in a cloth
Would I wait till I was dry
Would I be a butterfly
Would I live, would I die?

Lesley Wilson, 8 years

10

I may be

I may be small
   But my hands have known mountains.
      I may be small
         But my feet tread this whole world.
            I may be small
               But my body has stood before the setting sun.
                  I may be small
                     But the light-filled universe
                     Shines in my eyes.
                  I may be small
                  But within my soul dwells divinity.
               I may be small
            And stretches past mountains
         This world,
      This setting sun,
   Our universe and divinity.

A.J. Ordonez

11

The woods

The woods,
Dense with trees,
Surrounded by wire.
I`alone know the entrance.

I'm familiar
With the pathways,
And acquainted with the animals;
The overlord of my kingdom.

In my world,
The trees and the wire
Belong to me.
Who dares to touch them?

That trespasser would say:
'Hey, clear off!'
What does he know?
He only owns it.

John Perry, 12 years

12

The island

The island
Lies
Desolate,
Unexplored,
Untouched by anyone
But me.

The island
Is
My island,
My property,
My hideout...
I'm Adam here.

Yet
What is this?

Litter?

John Perry, 12 years

13

My own

It's mine.
I own it.
A secluded spot
Where nobody goes,
Ever.
Except me.

After an event:
A household tragedy,
I go there to think aloud to myself
About what might have been.

Here,
Many of history's greatest plans
Are made.

Like a castaway
On an island,
I am isolated:
Cut off from civilisation.
At this place,
A place not even my friends know about.

A place where only the trees can hear.

John Perry, 13 years

14

Longshoredrift

When it's rained a lot then clear again,
In the puddles along my road
Hang bright rainbows in muddy grey,
Bits of sky pebble-rippled.
Mysterious visions of rainy day reality.

So let's lose ourselves in puddles
And float into reflection
Transcending all our troubles
To find the true direction
Of the road we're on.

When we've voyaged out then in again,
Among the quiet waters of the mind
Project liquid lights on matter grey,
Gentle being thought-rippled.
Deepening shadows of vast eternity.

So let's look deep into our souls
And divine the right direction
Penetrating the inner veil
With fathomless reflection
On the road we're on.

When it's night-misty out then bright again,
In the moisture on your hair
Are golden droplets down dripping,
Fragmented mirrors sun-refracting.
Sunshine rites along the shores of being.

Then we'll radiate within ourselves
Flashing deep into our essence
Transcending drifting reams of dreams
To find the cosmic irridescence
Within the road we're on.

Jonathan Matthews, 18 years

15

Inner world

I pull down the blinds
Of my eyes,
And release the waiting thoughts.
My thoughts are of fields of ripe corn,
Swaying in the wind.
Of lions
Who run faster than a car,
And leap higher than a horse.
I am transported to another world,
A world in which
There are no rules,
No restriction or barriers.
A world where there are no watchful eyes
Always looking for faults
And criticising.
In this world,
People go barefoot,
And the sun shines continually
Day and night.
I am in a world
Where locks and keys
Have no place,
And freedom dominates,
In my Inner World.

Susan Farish, 12 years

16

Sonnet

When God created Adam out of clay
Placing him east of Eden long ago,
He little thought what kind of race would grow
To shame the man he moulded on that day,
But took the rib while sleeping Adam lay
As if he were determined we should know
The truth his son would live and die to show,
Though from the first we could not keep God's way.
Better for all if he had stayed his hand,
Leaving the beasts as keepers of his land;
Through ages men have fought with upward gaze,
Tributes of blood to deities unknown,
Confused by hearts that hold a need to praise
With minds that mock simplicity outgrown.

Margaret Portch, 17 years

Responses

17

I wonder

I wonder, I wonder, I wonder why,
Why sun and moon are up so high.
Oh I wonder, I wonder,
How does it thunder?
It makes me frightened when it lightens.
I wonder how moths
Make silk cloths.
I wonder how it changes from day to night
And how it changes to morning light.
I wonder how fishes swim in the sea
And how we get honey from the bee.
I wonder how we shout and talk
And how we run and how we walk.
I wonder, I wonder, I wonder why,
Why sun and moon are up so high.

Julie Rains, 10 years

18

Questions

Where do words go when we speak?
Why do seven days make a week?
Where does the light of the sun go at night?
Why is the moon's light never so bright?
How can the flowers break through the ground?
How do they know there is no snow around?
How do the dark clouds change into rain?
What makes the clouds dark and then white again?
How many questions can there be?
As many as there are fish in the sea.

Karen Jones, 9 years

19

Stress of life

O, the effort of being born,
Lungs expanding, first breath drawn.
O, the strain of trying to walk,
And the frustration of learning to talk.
O, the wonder of childhood eyes,
O, the torture of teenage whys.
Knowing the difference between right and wrong,
And the nightmares of the hydrogen bomb.
Rush, tear, noise and clamour,
Deadens all this so-called glamour.
O, the agony of first love spurned,
O, the joy of love returned.
O, the stress of family life,
Worry, work, toil and strife.
Then when all have left the fold,
What is left?
Despair of growing old.

Christopher Pinch

20

Gift for a child

I wish this child to have a gift —
Perhaps of love?
And if it is granted
Love may turn, its other side is hate
And hate brings men to war
And mothers mourn.

Perhaps for art?
To paint a masterpiece in paint or words,
Inspire young fools to fight
And burn the dead within their doors!

Perhaps of intelligence?
This gift of life could lead a man to search
And find — a way of death
So vast, so terrible,
My earth may be destroyed!

Perhaps the skill to build?
But bombs and missiles with blasphemous names
Are built —
From building rockets to conquer space,
To building bombs to conquer man —
Even this gift may turn to sin!

Perhaps the gift to learn
To live with other men
To learn to love the life we have
To learn kindness
And crush war and suffering with love —

So, love is the answer
The best gift
The gold of life.

Robert Bramley, 15 years

21

King and God

I am the
   man
   who is called
      Love
I am King
   and God
   to starry-eyed
      Lovers
      under 21
   walking along
   the fish quay
      seeing the golden sand
      and not the scum
smelling the sweet perfume
   and not the stinking fish
   picking flowers
      in old air raid shelters
      and seeing nothing
   yet seeing more
   of what really matters
      than everyone else
      and I am unseen
unpalpable
   and not unreal
   I am real
      to those
      who know I'm there
   and to them
   I am King
      and God
and
   everything
   and All
      and nothing
and
   living and breathing
   dreaming and scheming
      seeing and being
      me the One and Immortal
   King and God.

      Paul McCarthy, 16 years

22

How, at the age of twenty-five, I shall find true happiness

Somewhere,
lives the pretty girl
I shall marry.

Somewhere,
stands the church
where we will be photographed
with all our relatives
and great Aunt Ada.

Somewhere,
is the bank
which will give me my mortgage.

Somewhere,
is the coastal town,
where we will go for our Sunday drives
in the middle of winter.

Somewhere,
when this happens,
I shall take out my brain,
solemnly bury it,
and read a funeral service over it,
for I will no longer need it.

Paul Sutton, 16 years

23

The coin

I was wandering in the meadow,
Eyes lowered,
Staring at the dead brown hay,
When something caught my eye.
I stooped, picked it up,
And saw it was a coin,
Old and timeworn.
I rubbed it on my sleeve, and wandered on,
And as I went I saw the wealth of empires,
Crumbling, falling,
'Til all that remained was my coin,
Small, dirty and insignificant,
The last remnant of a forgotten hoard.

Elizabeth Thomas, 14 years

24

The old barn

I discovered myself walking into a barn, an old barn, disused, nothing
   left,
Only a few loose bales of hay and some tools and a lamp.
A wooden crate holding them all.
The wooden walls charred,
A fire probably the cause of its abandonment.
Even so, the hay is in perfect condition.
A barn owl speaks to its mate.
The hay is comfortable.
I nestle down.
Dust slides down a shaft of sunlight that pierces the crumbling walls.
All is quiet.
Suddenly the barn is humming with a thousand questions,
That nuzzle into my ear.
How many cows have served their life here?
How many owls have kept sentry?
How many rainy nights, sunny days has this old barn witnessed?
Which farmer handled those tools and went out on a dark night with
   that lamp?
Then I realise that this old barn is not utterly desolate,
But a warm and lively storehouse of memories.

Joseph McKie, 13 years

25

To school

The day outside was
damp, drizzly and dull
    and
cold and cloudy and soggy
and wet like a wet sheet
just been hung up
and my face was long with misery
as if my face had just been hung up.
It was quiet and misty
and I was lost.
I was plodding along as if
I had my dad's shoes on.
I was half asleep, dozy, yawning
Still finishing my dreams.

Charles Mills, 13 years

26

Assembly

Cold, dreary, something uninteresting.
Look out of the window.
Dull and uninterested.
Fidget, bored, sleepy, dreary.
The teacher steps smartly on the front of the stage
Holding sheets of paper
Looks at us
Tries to look important.
Choir spring to their feet.
Piano, out of tune, like thunder.
I do not join in.
Dream!
Sometimes I pay attention to the notes.
Relief when we are dismissed,
Glad to go to lessons.
Feel sick in assembly.

Stephen Groombridge, 16 years

27

Right or wrong?

The chalk squeaks on the board.
The clear-cut, pure white strokes
Stare back from a black void.
They are full of meaning, yet incomprehensible;
They are perfect and correct in a world of wrong.
Is this all there is to life?
An equation; a sentence; the Ten Commandments?

The late afternoon sunlight plays on the wall.
I glance out of the window.
Nothing moves.
All is perfect, quiet and still.
Yet somewhere, miles away,
A young soldier's life is suddenly brought to an end.
And the teacher's voice drones on...

Elisabeth Essex

28

Boring lesson

Monotonous words lingering on
In one ear out the other
A quiet yawn and back to sleep.

Susan Linforth, 12 years

29

Our world of pop

The everlasting cries
And sounds of sobbing —
We came here for him,
And maybe to risk our only lives —
But why should we care?
We have the life we want,
Our world of pop.

But we know
We will never feel him;
He is famous
And we are plain;
For he stays
In a secret world of pop.

On your walls in the night
You can watch his longing face
As in a mirror, fading away
To a dream of you and him
In your only world of pop.

Kate Beven-Baker, 10 years

Feelings

30

Love

From love comes birth,
From birth we receive love,
Growing we give and receive love,
Suddenly, love is everything.
We crave to have more,
We yearn to give everything,
Love becomes a way of life,
Always giving and receiving.
Settling down we look less effervescent
But beneath the surface love grows stronger.
It lasts all of life
And still waits for us at the end.

Mary Wakelin, 14 years

31

From that faith, that rock
Which the hail
Of mockery and scorn
Cannot weather,
On which stands
That hope, that joyous hope
Which never allows despair,
Springs the flowing fountain
Which, quenching the fiery flames
Of anger,
Can offer only forgiveness.
Love...

Stuart P. Scott, 17 years

32

Happiness

Happiness is a wonderful feeling.When I am happy I have a feeling deep inside, it is like a volcano about to erupt, but it never does. Most times when I feel happy is when I have just got out of bed, I think that none knows what happiness is. It is really a feeling indescribable, a fabulous feeling. Sometimes I get so happy that I try to hold the happiness back and just smile. The happiest day of a year to me is Christmas. I have never ever not been happy on Christmas Day. When I wake up on Christmas Day the feeling in me bursts just like a big balloon.

Philip Cooper, 11 years

33

When I am happy I sometimes feel nervous and I get a tummy ache and sometimes I go mad I am jolly and I am merry sometimes I feel like I want to sing a song and I feel very funny and my mouth waters when I go mad I do head over heels and run round the room.

Claire Dorer, 6 years

34

The sound of the sea on weather worn rocks.
Lying in sun drenched bracken.
Climbing the fells in the misty morning.
Swimming in the cool clear ghylls and tarns.

The smell of tar.
Playing games in fresh green fields.
Listening to the sound of the wind
whistling in the gorse and the sound of birds.

As I return home in the evening
the greetings of my dog.
The lavish licking of his warm
tongue against my face.

Graham Kitchen, 11 years

35

Lost: A prayer in the void

The wind moans
The rain sobs
But the heavens are not weeping for me.
I love him
But he loves her
   The simplest situation ever to be.

Sunday
It's Sunday
Distantly the church bells are ringing
Songs of praise
On the air
Windy gusts of fervent hymn singing.

Where are the hills
from whence cometh my help?
There is only a plain
A flat desert of despair
I have never been so alone
There is nothing at all out there.

                 Anon, 17 years

36

Movement

I ran to the beach
 The sky was clear
The sea was blue
 And I was glad

I ran on the sand
 With the sea at my feet
And the stones all smooth
 And I was free

I kicked off my shoes
 And I laughed
I touched the water with my
 Bare pink toes

My feet sprang away
 As if to say
Don't go in
 But I did

The water lapped
 At my ankles edge
And I heard the gulls
 Cry overhead

I ran from the sea
 To a pool
And there the baby shrimps
 Tickled my feet

I ran from the sea
 To the dunes
Where the harsh green grass
 Felt hard against my feet

So I ran to a place
 Where the sand was soft
And I wallowed in the sun
 I felt peace

Then up I got and ran
 While the sand blew up
On my legs and my hair
 Fell across my face

I was glad as I ran along
 And the sea lapped at my
Pink cold toes
 I was free!

I leapt to the air
 I jumped to the sky
And heard the gulls cry
 You're free.

Fiona Maclaine, 10 years

37

Paradise

I am running:
Running through a yellow cornfield.
I am walking:
Walking along a dusty pathway.
I am dodging:
Dodging the trees in a wood.
I am kicking:
Kicking the stones on a road.
I am looking:
Looking at the lonely, wandering clouds.
I am free:
Free from routine; free from the world.

John Perry, 13 years

38

The wide, wide world

The world is wide
There's no place to hide
There is no way out
I look round and about
I go to school every day
And learn my sums the proper way.
Then when I go out to play
I try to get out another way
But now I know there's no way out
Although I still look round and about.

Louise Hillyer, 8 years

39

Shame

I have never been so ashamed.
  Hiding under cover,
  I was afraid to be seen
    By People.

I hated them.
  They caused my humiliation,
  They were to blame.

It was not my fault.
It was never my fault.
  They enlarged
    Petty issues,
    Gross exaggerations.

It was they who caused it;
  My shame.
    Dark corners,
    Insignificant alcoves,
      Became havens
      For the hunted.

Searched for
  To be scorned and laughed at,
  To be humiliated.

Pairs of eyes,
  Staring and prying,
  So that they could see for themselves.

Incessantly I tried not to notice,
  Trying not to feel,
    As they stared and glared...
      To humiliate.

          Stephen Bateman, 15 years

40

When I got angry

When I got angry I started to shout,
And it seemed like steam rushing out of a kettle.
I tried to stop myself but I couldn't.
I was so angry I wanted to hit
Someone or something.
Then my mother talked to me
But she made me angrier.
I was so angry sweat was pouring off my face.
Then suddenly everything went black
Then it came light again.
And once again I was my normal self.

Linda Newnham, 14 years

41

A failure

We were talking,
Just talking normally as girls do.
I forget what it was about,
Nothing important.
Then, the subject changed,
We were talking about God.

At first I just listened,
Not expecting to hear what I did.
They were insulting Christians,
They were insulting my friends and myself,
They were swearing at me.
Their remarks struck me like knives,
They pulled at my heart strings.

I didn't say anything,
I didn't defend my friends.
I didn't defend God above all.
I just stood there,
They laughed and walked away.

I felt so guilty, so much as if I had let my side down,
I could have cried but I didn't,
I couldn't,
I felt so ashamed.
I could have walked away,
Not listened ... But no.

How could I tell my friends?
How would they feel?
I didn't have to tell God, he knew.

I knew he forgave me, but could I forgive myself?
Or could they forgive me?
I had failed the test.

Why?

Was it because I had no faith,
no courage, no confidence, no love?
A question time will answer for me.

Pam Sephton, 15 years

42

The unborn child

Before birth
I felt nothing
I knew nothing.
I was produced
Miraculously
In a small
pocket of flesh
that was part of me.
I lived and yet
was not born.
I was dormant
yet unawakened.
I was safe
Inside my pocket of flesh.
I knew nothing.
I felt nothing
and yet
I was on the threshold
of something
I did not understand
and slowly yet suddenly
I was born into light.
Yet the light
came through shut eyes,
and I was afraid.

Barbara Blake, 15 years

43

When I grow up

When I grow up I will be a housekeeper and I will have a nice pinny on me and I will have a nice dress on   But I will not have boys for children I will have two girls for my children   I will cook the dinner and I will get a shopping bag and go to the shops and buy things   Sometimes I can have a rest and when the children come home I will make the tea and I will make the tea for my little dog now   I wash the clothes Monday and I will go shopping Wednesday   My husband will be untidy and he will pick me a job and I will say pick up your own newspapers and put the telly on yourself   Now he comes in my living room with muddy boots so when he comes in he has to have his shoes on   He will have dark hair and a tidy jacket on he takes the dog for a walk and puts the children to bed.

Andrea Lamb, 6 years

44

When I am Big

When I am Big I will get married. I will have a white dress. I will get married in Keswick. I will get maried to christopher. I will have some bridesmades. I will invite my friends to my wedding. it will be sunny it will be exciting. when you get maried you get some flowers and a husband there will be a vicar there and he will conduct the people who are singing to you. There will be a red carpet on the floor so you wont dirty your dress. my wedding will be exciting. when I am married I will be called Mrs Sian Hayes.

Sian Rothwell, 6 years

45

Rising thirteen in the sands of time

The scorching sun beats down upon the sand,
Mirages appear and disappear before my eyes.
Buckets and spades are far away upon burnt rocks, in shade.
The sunbeams are hazy. I cannot capture them to make a way clear.
I'm rising thirteen in the sands of time,
The distant mystic roar of an eternal tide
Echoes the new rhythm I feel in my blood.
The sands stretch, but a misty cloud shrouds the horizon.
What is beyond?

Judith Powell, 12 years

46

Thirteen, our great secret

When you're thirteen
You have ideas which you can't tell
Anyone, no one, anymore
Not even your parents.
It's a secret you can't tell
Anyone, no one, no more.
They say you're too small
They would not understand
It's a pity they don't understand
Because
It's A Great Secret
Great Secret! Great Secret!

Bruna Basanese

47

Life

Life goes on around us
   With joy and mirth and tears,
Life goes on around us,
   Through all the passing years.
What have I done so far?
   What is there to do?
I have all my memories,
   What is there in view?

   Shall I be a teacher?
   Shall I be a nurse?
   Shall I be a doctor?
   I could do far worse!
   Will I be a beauty?
   Will I be a hit?
Were I to be a linguist?
   Shall I be a hit?
Shall I go to college?
   Should I stay at home?
   What if I should marry?
   What if I should roam?

What will the future bring me?
   How is one to know?
Who can ever fathom
   How far there is to go?
Life goes on around us,
   With joy and mirth and tears,
Life goes on around us,
   Through all the passing years.
                  Jenny Cox, 13 years

48

Time

Time means everything to me.
Time past, time present, time future
Ordains my life.
I read and learn of kings and empires long ago.
The Roman road I walk along
Is an echo of long ago
Time, locked in museums of relics and dry scrolls.

Time is present to me *now*
What I do and say and think
I cannot hold and keep one single second
As I write this the moment has passed.

My hands stretch out to the future.
Is it bright with promise for me?
Please God, make my future a great adventure.
For life is short to me.
The future will soon be the *present*
And one day I shall be old
Gnarled and broken like a blighted tree.

Pamela Scurr, 11 years

49

Today or tomorrow I will be here
Waiting
Waiting for something:
An answer,
An answer to all my questions.
So far they've all been lies.
They seem the truth until I discover something new,
Something I was not aware of before.
But maybe there isn't an answer,
I mean, one only,
Because it seems the way you look at it, the answer changes,
The reason changes,
And everything is seen in a different light.

Anon, 14 years

50

Recollection

In the darkest cavern of my mind,
I dredge the shadows,
Try to recollect.
To find,
Particles of memories
Grab the dust
Feel around the darkness
Rub the moistness from my eyes
And run through the lost episodes of time,
But trip and fall
And all is lost,
For a moment,
Then I try again.
With aching mind
I tap the forbidden
Barrel of distilled fantasy,
And am left at last
With a clear beautiful vintage wine,
But now it is too distant
To be relevant
To me.

Catherine Hodgson, 12 years

51

A prayer

Dear Jesus, make me like what you were when you
were six years old.

An Indian boy, 6 years

52

Growing up

No longer
The welling up of condensed sorrow,
The trickle of warm, saline beads
Mounting...
Nor the gasping sob
Reaching deep into mucous caverns
And shuddering back again,
Sucking once more,
Throwing the tickling tear arcing silently
And more slide down the gleaming channel
Tremulous and hot
Heaving deep into the shaking body
Out into every pulsing vein
Till the raging wanes and there is
Only
A sweet aspen moaning.

Now just the taut cerebralisation of anguish
And a dry throat croak.

D.J. Kidd, 16 years

53

End of term

Today there has been too much
Current running through us
Too many electrons beating through the air
In the morning we trooped sober
To the assembly hall
Sang our hymn, recited 'to give and not to count the cost...'
And wondered if we'd given enough
Then they brought him on to the corner of the stage
Grown suddenly old and grey
There were speeches and too many thanks and tributes but
No tears
And the poppies glowing red on the sides of the white cups
... for remembrance and 'constructive good living'
(a Chinese phrase)
Then we went back to the little square blue room at the top
For the last time
To purge it of ourselves
Books, papers, clothes, binned or pinned or
satchelled away until
It was bare and austere as a cell
Then the bell
Rang again and we went by its summons
Down into the square tarmaced courtyard.

Jean Teasdale, 16 years

Family

54

What is a mum?

A mum is somebody who looks after you. She buys you clothes, food and shoes. She also buys you toys. She tidies the house, does the dishes, cleans the floor, does the beds, makes the breakfast, makes the dinner, makes the supper, dries the dishes, washes the clothes, dries the clothes, irons the clothes, goes down street for the shopping, gets the biscuits, gets the bread, gets the butter, gives you your pocket money, makes the fire, keeps the house nice and warm, gets the eggs, gets the tomatoes. She also gets you presents for Christmas and your birthday. I love my mam very much and she loves me.

Ronald Smith, 10 years

55

Our baby

The nurse told us to come and see the baby. It had black hair and when Mammy put it in the cot it went to sleep. We waited for a little while. The baby put its little fingers out of its cardigan. then it opend its eyes. It smiled at Julian and went back to sleep. I am going to buy something for the baby and I will go and see it. The baby has got a bandage round his rownd thing to keep it in. The baby is a boy. He has some woollen balls in his cot to play with. He has a little thumb.

Kevin Clark, 7 years

56

A child's view of a happy family

Our family is a happy one, but we have our little arguments now and then. I like my parents, but I like my mum best because she always understands me, but I still like my dad because he helps me with my homework and tells me things I don't know. Really my dad is small compared with my uncles. He has not got a lot of hair on his head and he has a peculiar nose. Also he has a tubby body and small feet. But he has a lovely character and really is kind.

My mum is generous and kind although she is often strict, but then all mothers should be. She has curly hair with grey streaks here and there. She always has a lot of housework to do to try and keep the house tidy and clean for when the family comes home, and she should be proud of the results because it always looks spotless.

Now my brother is a teenager, and he's a terror, but mother keeps saying he has a soft spot but she can't find it. His hair is curly like my mum's, but my dad says it's like a mop. We are always arguing over little things and big things and I must say he has a very hard punch.

Now about myself. I myself am very argumentative. I have fair hair not very long and my mum says it needs cutting but I don't think it does. In school I am always getting told off. I have a good part in me but it won't come out of me.

But as I said before we are a happy family and we hope it stays like that for a very long time to come.

Susan Day, 10 years

57

November evenings

Going home from school on a Friday evening
I put my scarf and gloves on
And my mac, it's cold outside
It has been a typical November day
In the morning a sharp cold frost filled the air
The sky was clear then.
But grey, heavy, damp storms blew across the sky
Now there's a blanket of yellow, clammy vapour filling the air
Streets' lights shine through the smoky haze.
I meander along, hardly caring how long I take.
Even though I am cold — cold, yes very cold!
Suddenly I wish that I was at home
I think of my house lit up and warm
Then I think of television
I begin to run, thinking about home
I run around the corner into our road
I see my house and run even faster
I cross the road
I ring the doorbell energetically
My mother appears
She tells me off for ringing the doorbell too hard.
I take no notice!
The warm air hits me like a gust of wind
I rush into the sitting room and switch on the television
I lie back in my chair, now I am warm. Great I am home!

Marianne Beeks, 11 years

58

The generation gap

'Do you have to leave your room in such a mess, and do you have to pin up those ghoulish pictures; I do think a nice country scene would be quieter, how you can sleep with all those faces looking down at you, I don't know. My mother would not let me pin up pictures, it just ruins the wallpaper. Do you have to slurp that tea, do sit up straight, you'll get round shoulders. I wish you would not go out with that light thing on, another waste of money, you just don't know how lucky you are, when I was young...' I stare out of the window, leaving my mother's voice far behind me in our little semi-detached council house.

I have learned to shut her voice out, maybe it's wrong I know, but everything seems to be wrong in our generation, nothing that can be put right through talking or listening. Where there are different ages and different thoughts, there will always be differences of opinion. To me it's like walking on two opposite banks of a river, and since there is no bridge, there is no way of getting across. If we try to swim we will be dragged away by the strong current. We are flowing in the same direction but taking different paths, and this is the way it will always be, until someone discovers a way to stay young.

I wonder if I will become like my Mum, afraid of insecurity, afraid of things changing. They are afraid of the new world and its possibilities. They cannot grasp the idea that people change. I look at her face lined with worry, anxiety, and I feel sorry for her, and try to understand.

Anon

59

Me!

If anyone's in trouble,
it's Me!
If the cat's got no milk,
it's Me!
If a knife drops, or a door bangs,
it's Me!
Me! Me! Me!
it's always Me!

      If Mum goes out, who minds the baby?
      Me!
      If the baby starts screaming,
      it's Me!
      If the fuse is broken,
      it's Me!
      Me! Me! Me!
      it's always (guess who!)
      ME!

                 Susan Stowe, 11 years

60

Family

Our holiday
Sun and sea,
Sand and grass.
    Suntan lotion
    Ice cream.
        Good food and fun.
They bind us together — yet
Already I am apart.
    I walk ahead
    And love the crashing sea.
They linger,
Watching fish basking in the river.
They are all I have,
    Yet of my own free will
      I will soon leave
Family...

                 Anon

61

Mother and daughter

'Stay out till eleven?
Certainly not!
At your age
I was in by eight
In bed by nine.'

'At your age I was...'
Same old notes
I only asked one simple question,
And I get past history.

'But my friends...'
'Your friends aren't my children.
I have responsibilities,
It's for your own safety.'

'I can look after myself,
I'm fifteen now...'
'The way you act,
Anyone would think you were nineteen.
Can't you realise how I care for you?
I'm not doing it for spite,
There is a reason!'

A reason,
An explanation,
They all mean the same,
Reach the same conclusion:
I'm just too young.

Jayne Howard, 16 years

Relationships

62

Dumb words

I looked —
  And wondered if those
    Penetrating eyes,
      Smiling, appreciating and answering
        Every spoken question in the
          Crowded, smoke filled room
          Could intercept and decipher
            The unspoken yet urgent question
            My eyes were asking you?

Ann Hunter

63

A meeting

Into the city you run.
People laugh, they think it's fun;
All turn and stare as you run past,
All wondering why you're running so fast.

Will you get there on time?
You make it, and realise how fine
It is to be alive, and to feel the sun.
When he approaches, you know you've won
The battle against time, just once.

Into the crowds you mingle, slowly moving,
Both your faces alight and glowing.
He keeps hold of your arm tightly,
Laughing with you,
Then, hugging you lightly.

He walks you home, nice and slow,
Neither wanting the other to go.
'Pick you up at half past eight.'
He leaves, kissing lightly over the gate.

Jean Killett

64

Chance game

How do I know your love is true?
How do I know I can trust you?
I never will, but I sometimes do. Silly me
To have such doubts. I should just believe.
You said you'd meet me at half past eight;
Supposing, through no fault of yours, you were late —
Me thinking you'd deliberately stayed away,
Not speaking, and being nasty to you next day.
But suppose I don't turn up on time?
Then the fault for love lost would be mine.
But if everything goes all right,
It should be a wonderful night.

Jean Killett

65

Don't you know?

Oh, you hurt me, you make me cry.
Why do you do so? I wonder why?
Do you do it on purpose or don't you see
How much even 'Good morning' means to me.
But sometimes you just grimace a smile,
Even that makes me content for a while,
But you go away, without a word or smile
And make me sad,
Feeling miserable and hurt inside. I must be mad
To even like you.

Jean Killett

66

Different people

Two brothers, how much alike I cannot tell,
The one not known, the other known so well.
What are their reactions — different or the same?
Maybe one life full of happiness, the other full of pain.
One stays at home, the other carefree.
Both need love, just like you and me.

Jean Killett

67

Now what happens?

Argument,
Confrontation
Of two ex-companions.

Friends —
At first,
But now: complete enemies.

Comrades
In childhood battles:
He and I were at the Alamo.

But time
Took its toll
Of our friendship.

Characters
Change;
We found ourselves separated,

Permanently.

John Perry, 12 years

68

An indictment

Boy, dragging dusty feet on dusty street —
Mouth hard set, alone, by friends deserted.
Childhood friends, school friends, have all forgotten?
'What has turned you from me? I am unchanged —
We played together on this dusty street.

What have I done that you should neglect me?
Well — I don't care, it's too late to be sad.
"No place for coloureds" they told me last week,
So I'm not conforming — why bother to try?
Is it just you feel forced to reject me?'

On to a place which is classed as a home,
But he is not ever there at his ease.
He does not know the country they talk of —
He was born here, in this Christian town.
When, if ever, will he know a real home?

'We're not prejudiced here, of course, just look
At situations in countries abroad,
You're lucky to be here at all', they say,
'Where else should I be but in my home town?
And I say there's somewhere else they should look'.

Lights going out in all of the houses —
As they will in this coloured boy's eyes soon.
Darkness is descending on the city.
As black as the hatred which will be born.
Hope is needed in all people's houses.

Boy, dragging dusty feet on dusty street,
Despair clouds the horizon everywhere
How has the meaning to life slipped away?
Where are the people so kind and so just?
Is colour a reason for treatment like this?

Esme Glauert, 16 years

69

Conversation in November

You spoke of partings:
I, of foxes' trails through snow
and ashen birds
winging thread-drawn on
November skies.

You spoke of solitude:
and I of rattling grass
frost dried on the crackling path
and white-rimmed leaves
curled on brittle stems.

You spoke of sorrows:
I, of hands pushed deeper
into throbbing warmths of pockets
fingers cold with speaking
gestures on to chilly air.

You spoke of dying:
then I was silent —
torn between growing shadows
and the snowflakes
melting in your hair.

Jan Walker, 17 years

70

In closing

In closing
might I ask

If we meet
sometime next year

Shall we smile
as friend

Or shall we stumble
over memories
and be confused?

Jane Elliot

71

Loneliness

Alone in the world:
    Deaf,
who can not hear.
    Blind,
who can not see.
    Dumb,
who can not speak.

Alone in the world:
    Sick,
who are kept in bed all day.
    Old,
who are widowed and lonely.
    Coloured,
who are different from others.

Alone in the world,
    They wait,
but no one comes.
    They wish,
but nothing comes.
    No visitors, no food, no help.
Alone in the world.

Judith Leon, 11 years

72

Old folk

Unfirm, unsteady,
Never, ever ready,
Old men, very heavy,
Old women, small and thin,
It would shock a king.

Transport is an essential thing,
No telephone to give a ring.
Bad health,
And with stealth
People ignore them.

The old men drink,
And sit and think.
Old women pause,
While doing their chores;
Unsteady legs.

No one to do repairs,
After all, who cares?
Can't afford bus fares,
It's like being caught in snares.

No family,
All in Italy,
Lying in the sun,
No thoughts of Mum.

They think of suicide,
Is now the time to decide?

Sitting in chairs,
Not able to brush their hair,
For no one cares.

The Church is supposed to be
   doing their thing,
But the doorbell never rings.

So cold,
Not able to hold
A cup to drink.
They sit and think
Of happy times,
So sad.

Nigel Forman, 13 years

73

Being old

I think it must be lonely and sad to be old,
the firelight flickering in front of you,
the rocking chair goes backwards and forwards
and the candle burns down slowly.

Michael, 9 years

74

Why should it be me?

You're out of work
They say you're a lout
You're on the dole
For nothing at all
You sit and laze
It's all the craze
You're bored to tears
With all your fears
No money to spend
With the kids to attend
The bills come in
No money in the tin
They'll have a job
Get no more than a bob
You draw your money
It's not very funny
Money for the kids
Money for the wife
Money to pay for the H.P.
Why should it be me?

Andre Bloyce, 15 years

75

Time

The passage of Time is constant.
Why, therefore,
Is it different things to many people?
The old lady,
Who spins her routine web,
Day after day, never seeing
The outside world.
And when time stops for her
Who knows?

The housewife,
Doing her daily weekly drudgery,
Feeling its oppression
Burn up her time.

The business man
Caught in the tangle of success ...
Money making money losing,
Ultimately time consuming.

The schoolboy
Who wants to be old
Before his time
Wants to escape the restrictive bond
But not its security.
'ALL IN GOOD TIME'.

And for me?

Time is confusing, teasing, lacking,
Wasted, gained, lost.

Now here, now gone,
When you're not there to share it with me ...

Anon

76

The white stick

Red bricks, grey slate, cream road.
My eyes ached,
Same old walls, same old houses,
Old churches, old shops, old railings,
Everything was old,
No grass or trees.
I was sick, for want of the country;
I looked around me.
My eyes were drawn
To a solitary figure, walking slowly.
I saw in the figure's hand a white stick.
Blindness.
I imagined the eternal blackness.
What had he done
To earn this mockery of man?
The figure turned into another street,
Tapping, feeling for the next shape,
Dependent on the white stick.
I wanted to help him.
What use was I? Just to show him the next corner.

Anon, 15 years

77

Thank you, God

I sat down in the park alone,
For peace and quiet on my own,
But then some noisy children came,
Screaming, shouting — almost insane,
Until at last I could not bear
To hear them shouting everywhere,
So I stood up about to shout,
'You little horrors, please get out!'
But then I saw a child so small,
And realised that she could not hear at all,
So the next time in your prayers, my dear,
Just thank the Lord that you can hear.

Caroline Astley, 11 years

78

My dream for Wolverhampton

If an immigrant woman is seen in the streets wearing her native clothes, passers-by will have all sorts of peculiar ideas about her. Some people may invariably think nothing of it. Others, presumably those who have nothing else to think about, may simply think she looks funny, and others still — and these in my opinion are the prejudiced, the people who look at things from one angle and one angle only — are led to believe that this woman's clothing is symbolic of the fact that she wants nothing to do with the native born of the country she is living in, that she wants to keep well and truly away from the people whose job she may be stealing, from whose shops she is buying her food and in whose houses she is snugly sheltered while the native born may still be desperately searching for somewhere to live. It is angered with these thoughts that these people are overcome with hatred and will indulge in anything to get rid of this woman whose character they may be mistaking anyway.

Let's look at it from another angle, from the immigrant's point of view. Let's dress this woman in English-type fashions. Even now a similar problem arises. Now the immigrants are going to think of her as something of a traitor, as someone who has taken advantage of her opportunity of living in another country, and, sharply leaving the customs she was taught, has developed new and frantic ideas.

So what do we dress her in? It should make no difference whatever — that is the whole point of writing this essay. I want people to learn that the cream of a person's heart is shown in the character. Not in the clothes she wears, not in the food she eats, not in the colour of her skin, but in her character.

Krishna Devi, 15 years

79

My dream for Wolverhampton

My hope for Wolverhampton is to see it one day a prosperous, happy mixed community.

You have only to walk down the street to see the many nationalities of people who live and have made their homes in Wolverhampton — South Africans, West Indians, Jamaicans and Pakistanis. It is not the first time we have seen many newcomers to Wolverhampton, for during the time of the Industrial Revolution people from all over the country flocked to the large towns in the Midlands. This was because there was little or no work in the north and south of England, Wales, Scotland and Ireland. These people over the years have become the Midlanders we know today. I hope that one day also our new immigrants will be accepted as Midlanders too.

Caroline Lucas, 15 years

80

The number eight

The number eight
Rolled to a stop by the concrete shelter.
A negro embarked,
And people stared for a split second
Then returned to their talking,
But more quietly.
He sat beside a woman, who turned away
To stare with cold embarrassment through the window.
Suddenly a little boy turned in his seat,
And asked, 'Why are you black?'
' 'Cos I spent a lot of time in the sun,' replied the negro.
No one laughed.
He smiled.
Then sat, ashamed.

Alan Rodgers, 17 years

81

Mentally-handicapped children

First I will say how terrible it is to be mentally handicapped. If you are a blind man you can still hear beautiful sounds, if you are deaf you can see wonderful things, if you are dumb, you can see and hear, and sometimes dumb people can be taught how to speak. But if you are mentally handicapped you cannot learn properly, because of your brain.

Christine Joan Barber, 10 years

82

A mentally handicapped child may eventually become an adult in body, but still only have the mentality, outlook and unstable behaviour of a small child. He is still a human individual and we must help him to make the best out of his life.

Richard Michael Goodwin, 10 years

83

Can't move
Needs freedom,
As though a gate of life and freedom
closed
Alone.
Wondering, wandering.
A world of their own.
A leaf drops unnoticed in the water.
Dying for love.
People stare like scarecrows.
Lost,
like a traveller being lost
In a desert.

Kathryn Barwick, 10 years

84

Often I despair
When I explain what she must do
She shows no interest. And yet the smiles
Like the warm sun breaking through an all too doubtful view of blue
Excite me hopelessly to demand she is a saint among sinners
Wandering too pure to understand what harm can come to her
If I don't run and hold her hand.

Patricia Daniel, 15 years

85

Sarah

There,
By the ever-closed window,
She stands, lost
In the maze of thoughts, which,
Meaningless as her speech,
Condemn her.

Trapped in the present of her past
Unmoved
By the tragic non-existence of her future
She is condemned and abandoned
By the society that has locked her
In the stony prison of her mind.
A society
Which does not care.

There,
Blinded by pain and mental anguish
Sarah lives and laughs,
Suffers and smiles,
Waiting for the morning
Which will never come.

Stuart P. Scott, 18 years

86

Johnny Williams

Lonely's the life that Johnny Williams leads,
Love and affection are his greatest needs.

Poor Mrs Williams, she labours away,
Father's a businessman, no time to play,
So Johnny is left alone most of the day,
It's no wonder he's lonely when things go this way.

Johnny is twelve, but he seems nearer three.
His babyish bouncing is scaring for me,
Little boys run, when he wants them to stay,
Because of his size, and the way that he'll play.

Aidan John Semmens, 10 years

87

Hunger

Hunger hurts,
It· stings inside,
There's a hole in my stomach,
It's very very wide.

There's my meal,
Beans and bread.
But before we eat,
The animals are fed.
Hunger hurts,
It stings inside.
There's a hole in my stomach,
It's very very wide.

We have one meal a day,
Then a painful wait
For the next spoon of beans
On an old tin plate.
Hunger hurts,
It stings inside.
There's a hole in my stomach,
It's very very wide.

The animals are thin,
But we are too.
But whatever happens,
We're going to get through.
Hunger hurts,
It stings inside.
There's a hole in my stomach,
It's very very wide.

Jacqueline Skinner, 12 years

88

Lullaby

hush my little baby
rest:
there's not much milk
left in my breast
there's not much milk
left in the world
that's why we starve
— for kindness —

hush my little baby
rest:
we'll wait here, soon
— perhaps it's best —
we'll not see the grey day dawning

Anon

89

Hunger

Hollowness,
Nothingness,
Feels like your stomach has vanished
Giving up hope,
Utter despair, pleading hopelessly for food,
Fighting,
Killing for food, for survival,
Agony,
Queuing in hope for food,
Weak, thin, fragile,
Skin pulled and stretched over protruding bones.

Moth eaten,
Meek,
Under developed and poor,
Ignorant,
Devastated by hunger, reduced to nothing.

Robert Clements, 11 years

90

Home in Peru

My footsteps sounded hollow on the sun-drenched cobbles,
The noise echoed; lonely between the white-washed walls,
I walked on, over the filth-spattered stones, grasses sprouting
    erratically between them.
The heat hung around the back street, smothering, oppressive,
Like a sodden blanket randomly discarded.
My shadow, jet black, walked with me over the peeling walls,
And over the hard, baked mud, over the front doors, over doorsteps,
And on down the street. A small girl was sitting in the sun,
Perched on the doorstep by an open door, her bare feet crossed,
Intent on something she held in her outstretched hands.
The child's clothes were dated, long, of thin cotton,
As were her petticoats. It would be her only clothing. On her arms,
She wore an old cloth coat far too small. Her dark,
Fine hair was braided at the back of her head. As I passed by,
On the other side of the street, I saw she was sewing,
With a thread of string, a cloth of shredded newspaper,
And no needle other than her fingers. She was making a toy.
The child's younger sister was sitting half in and half out of the
    aperture.
The sunlight framed her round, childish face in the gloom beyond.
Her chubby hands grasped the doorstep, and her unattended hair
Blew loosely in the breeze. Her black eyes looked appealing,
    beseechingly, at
Me, as I walked by, on the other side.

Julia Wise, 16 years

Rain

Heat,
shimmering,
scorching the
parched earch —
green blade forgotten.
Starving, powerless and
desolate, man crouches over
his empty bowl. Pain racks his
body; fear tears his mind. Unbeknown
the far horizon yields his hope — one
cloud no bigger than his emaciated fist
brings promise to this God-forsaken land.
New hope appears in his eyes; his mind already
dwells on the delights to come — the refreshing
coolness on his burning back, the hazy heat no
longer worrying his brow. Now his empty bowl lies
forgotten at his feet. Desolation disappears;
thunder throbs over the landscape — lightning
lashes the sky. He gazes at this miracle
unbelieving, yet knowing the reality.
This lonely man stares stupefied at
his hand where there lies, like a
beautiful pearl, the first drop
of reviving rain.

Clare Spelman, 13 years

92

Slums

Pollution — clogged air hangs outside boarded-windowed slums. Toothless old men and women stand on the doorsteps surveying dirty, bomb-terrain like streets. Brick lorries thunder along the road. The street is like a set of teeth, uncared for, dirty and lots of cavities. People are half-soaked and most of them are on the dole. Bone-revealing short haired mongrels scavenging in overturned bins and litter. Bulldozers and tractors are knocking down dangerous houses. Murphy's fish and chip shop stands next to a rubbish tip. The ladies are wearing brightly coloured hair rollers. It's a rats paradise.

Craig Seeley, 10 years

Creation

The birth of light

All was black: dark-velvet, deep-thick
    Aching softness, empty void;
— Frozen, heavy night.
Piercing winds slashed and cut the black in twain,
    Burning, bitter cold.

Greyness was born in the East.
    Slowly, slowly, blackest hills were seen,
Charcoal-pointed against a greying sky.

Iridescent almost-blackness formed an aurora round the earth,
Gnawing winds ceased and all was cloudy grey.

Pale light was in the sky:
    Transparent streamers; rippling waves.
Then came the Dawn,
    Jubilant Dawn, with her sister careful Sunrise,
        peeping shyly over templed hills.

All was light, gold-tarnished, shining splendour,
    A burst, a new awakening of dazzling pale brilliance.
Myriads of shimmering rays,
United to form one immortal Light.

Elspeth Adams, 14 years

94

Time

Who made time?
Was it God?
Yes! He made all things.
When did he make time?
Yes. When?

He created time at the beginning.
At the beginning of what?
At the beginning of time.
When was that?
Yes. When?

That was before time began.
What was there before?
Nothing, absolutely nothing.
Since when was there nothing?
Yes. Since when?

It was there all the time.

R.F. Enever

95

Hope in colour

Sunshine stealing softly,
Gently to my eyes,
And suddenly —
A new brilliance —
Colour.

Lying dormant
Woken by the dear old sun
Slowly-orange,
Splendid to eternity
Then, royal reds,
Richly radiant;
Proud purple — through to
Blue — true
Like summer skies.
And here and there
The slow sad greys
Of yesterdays.

There! golden yellow
Burstingly exuberant
A flash and gone.
Green-achingly emerald,
Life to the corn.
And russet brown
Singing of autumn.
And now and then
The slow sad greys
Of yesterdays.

And through my eyelashes
A myriad of flickering rainbows
Centred on sun.
So, in life.
Dimensions of colour.
Hopeful, fleeting glimpses
To bring us
Gay todays
And banish thoughts
Of sorrowful tomorrows
And slow sad greys
Of yesterdays.

Rachel Parbury, 16 years

96

What dark mysterious depths there
between land
and sky.

> *R.G.*
> *Written at 10.00 am on 3 March, 1975*

97

The sea

The sea is like a very very hungry giant, and it comes up and then goes back, and its feet come over the rocks and it eats the rocks all up. It eats the hills and it gnashes its barley-sugar teeth.

> *Anne Johnson, 6 years*

98

The sea roars and yells and humps its back up and plays.

> *Janis Ross, 5 years*

99

Waves during a storm

Lashing on the beach,
White horses riding high
In the moonlight night.

> *Clair Walker, 13 years*

100

Storm

It's thundering, it's raining
Water is falling from heaven
It's now very windy too.
The trees are moving, ready to walk.
Pieces of wood are banging against my window,
      trying to get in.
Everything is blowing about.

              Fleur Anderson, 8 years

101

A stormy night

Rushing, turning in the wind
The grass like sea,
The cows like boats,
The clouds are black and gloomy,
The lightning shows in the dark.

              Fleur Anderson, 8 years

102

On the beach

Water caressing the golden sands
Sea-horses jumping and prancing
Deep blue sea and sky both meet
I feel the sand beneath my feet.
Little waves trickle between my toes.
How I wish that I could go
Beyond the water where I'll find
The horizon which will bind
Together with the night.

              Phillippa Wilson, 11 years

103

Countryside

Flowers and trees,
Walls to the knees,
    Oak apples, thorns and briars,
I could stay looking out there
    For hours and hours.

F. Heighton, 7 years

104

The tree

The wind blows me backwards and forwards
Making my timbers creak.
If you listen carefully
You may hear me speak
Of lovers arm-in-arm
Standing in the shade,
Each person not really noticing me
As under my branches they laze.
The season changes my colour and size:
In winter, tall, thin and white, I look old and wise
Yet in the summer my branches are leafy and green.
Dressed in my many seasons I am
    Part of the natural scene.

Jean Killett

105

The tree

There it stood:
As tall as two houses.
Towering above the others of its kind,
Humbling itself only before the sky.

There it stood:
The intricate pattern of branches
Concealed beneath a mass of green leaves.

The whirring stopped.

A deafening silence broken by
The thud.

There it lay:
Leaving behind only the ugly stump.

John Perry, 13 years

106

Each spiralling sycamore seed
Could — with time — become a forest.

J.A.L.
Written at 10.00 am on 3 March, 1975

107

Looking out

I do not suppose there is much good
In a sparrow
But, in their brown business-like way
These little monks searching the ivy
On the arch and the turret
Know better than I, how to pray.

Jean Teasdale, 16 years

108

God made me
And I made a sandcastle
A model aeroplane and a car.
God made me and I made friends
With Ann and James and Tim.
God made me and gave
  me his power to make things.
God made me to go on with
  what he began.

Anon, 10 years

109

Song of a sportsman

The Lord created man with brain to help him enjoy life.
He gave man muscles and reflexes to kick, throw and catch a ball,
To dribble and shoot powerfully and accurately;
The eyes and anticipation to intercept a pass or shot;
The agility and speed to catch a ball in the air;
The sense to play fairly and try not to injure fellow players;
To remain calm and unruffled when an incident occurs and not to
        retaliate;
To do what he is told and abide by the expert's decision;
To stay in good humour whether he wins or loses,
And to be thankful that he can play at all.

John Bayley, 15 years

110

For God or man?

God has made everything:
  The iron ore in the ground,
The petroleum in the earth,
  The atmosphere around us,
And the atoms of which all these things are made.

But we have made
  Bullets from the iron ore,
Explosives from the petroleum,
  Gases from the atmosphere,
And bombs from the atoms.
  It is your world, God,
Please save us from these things.

D. Jordan, 14 years

111

Forgive us

Please forgive us, God,
With pollution and progress we have spoilt your world,
New buildings, smoky cities; if only we had cared.
With saw and hammer we chopped down your trees,
With sprays and fertilisers we killed flowers and bees.
We polluted the air with gases and smoke,
And wonder why we splutter and choke.
Fields used to be covered with grasses so sweet,
But now just greyness of bricks and concrete.
Papers and tins we threw in your beautiful blue lakes,
To make an improvement, thoughtfulness and care is all it takes.

Margaret Hutton, 14 years

112

Contrast

Unsightly factories bellowing out
Smoke, colouring the blue sky
Into a haze of grey.
Litter, turning the natural beauty
Of the countryside around,
Into a state of utter confusion.
Quiet running rivers and streams,
Turned into hazardous drains,
Harmful to both man and animals;
This is man's world.

Narrow winding streams in
Valleys; fields and meadows
On each side tinted golden with
Fresh, dew-covered buttercups.
Birds glide across the sky
Fluttering down like leaves
Off a tree in Autumn.
Mountains, each one completely different,
Containing wonderful qualities of their own;
This is God's world.

David R. Hazeldine, 14 years

Places

113

Cathedral Close

The cold Cathedral spire
Like a monolith razor-sharp
And vastly aloof in the blinking sunlight,
The point, crowning the mass of snow-laden pinnacles,
Is brought down to crisp, snow-flaked ground
By the Norman tower
Frost-bitten cold,
Standing stark against the pale sky.
The distant shouts of schoolboys
Disturb the eerie stillness.
The trees, stripped bare of warmth,
Hanging like glistening spider's webs,
On the still frozen air.
The snow, crackling and crunching with ice,
Is crushed underfoot
And left in the icy cold
To melt.

Matthew Johnson, 12 years

114

The city

Tears are trickling down the cheeks
of the leaves

The soft earth
Settles into a moist bed

Sleeping it breathes
Warmly

I walk, the pavement's wet

I don't know the Earth
Like that
Mother of my being

Ashes to ashes

At least we can see the sky.

Anon

115

Concrete jungle

Tall Sentinel flats,
Towering above the estate.
Cement, bricks, Slates,
Concrete, blocks, and frames,
Wide open spaces,
of green Scene,
Trees, and flowers,
Rows of houses.
Passage, alleys, lie between,
And the main road,
Splits the Concrete
Jungle in half.

Wayne Brereton, 10 years

116

Factories at night

God's silvery tapestry woven
across the sky
Sending beams of silvery spray
to each star
Carving out shapes of the
night.
Making them stand out
Blotting out impressive
moonlight
Outlining the factories
Making silhouettes out of them
All happening when we're
asleep in bed,
in our town at night.

Kathryn Langstaffe, 9 years

117

Icy white light
Ghostly carriage in the dark
An empty bus at night.

L.P.
Written at 10.00 am on 3 March 1975

118

Durham Cathedral

Tall towers reaching high
Almost touching the blue sky
If your secrets you could tell
What a story you would spell.
Stained glass windows
Heavy doors
Cuthbert's bones and cold grey floors.
Standing there for all to see
There for ever you will be.

Sarah Faulkner, 9 years

119

Pylons

They stand there
Year in
Year out
Quite an eyesore,
Stretching out to the horizon,
Looped together
As beads on a necklace,
But in their own way
They're a work of art —
Quite a modern piece of sculpture,
Static, never moving,
Passing electricity
From
Village to village
And
Town to town.
Power!

Julianne Radnedge, 12 years

Changing scene

My house down the old end was not what you call nice but to me it was great. I liked it because it was not hard to make friends. We played hopscotch in the entry.

Down the bottom of the garden was a toilet which when we played hide and seek we hid in. Down the road there was a waste area of land and every day my friends and I went there.

Tinkers always camped there and my mother would give us a penny to spend and the tinkers always gave us something.

We loved to play with the tinkers' children but now it's a shopping centre. All the houses down my road are all pulled down. The rag and bone man no more walks up and down in his cart taking rags and giving balloons. The cart was made out of wood and a white horse pulled the cart. We always went and stroked the horse which was very tired.

Up the side of the house grew ivy. Up the side of the doors and along the paths. Where the tinkers lived were old cars, frames of bikes; we played in the cars and we pretended we were going somewhere. 'All aboard??' we called when we played ships.

Tin cans, old boots we played with till it began to get dark and home we went, we were tired, dirty and happy.

When I got home my mother said *get* in that kitchen and have a good *wash*.

Susan Keys, 11 years

121

Scotland

Climbing rocks,
    Finding brochs,
Swimming lochs,
    Washing socks,
Eating baps,
    Taking naps,
Crossing ferries,
    Picking berries,
Finding bones,
    Collecting stones,
Seeing shells,
    Hearing bells,
Watching sheep,
    Fast asleep,
All together
    In the heather.

Susan Batty-Shaw, 10 years

The seasons

Year

Spring
Flowers blossom and bloom:
Yellow.
Trees
Preparing for summer:
A light green.
Nature and man
Ready to face
A new year.

Summer
Flowers fully grown:
Every colour.
Richer than spring.
Trees
Also
A rich dark green.
Blue skies
And men in white
Playing cricket.
Colourful spectators
Like 'liquorice allsorts'.
Watching the game.

Autumn
Flowers now scarce.
Trees: semi-bare:
Brown leaves
Withered and crisp
Waiting to fall.
The world all set for ·

Winter
No flowers.
No colour
Trees totally naked
Like skeletons:
Once alive
Now dead.
The world seeming
So joyless ...
Until
Suddenly:

Spring
Flowers blossom and bloom:
Yellow.
Trees
Preparing for summer:
A light green.

John Perry, 12 years

123

Summer

Summer is a beautiful time
Lots to do in the hot sunshine
In the fields the green grass grows
By the stream the water flows.
Flowers pop up and begin to peep
Wild animals wake up from their sleep.
Leaves begin to grow on trees
And flying around are busy bees.
In summer we have hot sunshine
I wish it was like it all the time.

Julie Rains, 10 years

124

The summer storm

Hot is the air and clear the sky,
　All is close and still;
The new-mown grass looks brown and dry,
　The gay flowers droop and die.
The dog lies sprawling, panting,
　The bird sits with open bill,
They know a summer storm is brewing.
　Soon there comes a distant rumbling,
A black cloud gathers in the west,
　Sweeps darkly, slowly across the blue.
Thunder crashes, lightning flashes,
　Splits the frightening gloom in two.
The rain falls faster, faster, faster,
　Man and beast run for shelter,
Thankful for the cool, wet air.
　And after, when the cloud has passed,
A new world glistens in the sun.
　The grass looks green, the flowers brighter,
The dog jumps and is full of fun,
　Everything smells fresh and new —
Fresh hope brought by the wind that blew.

Mary Morris, 12 years

125

Autumn

Autumn is here bursting with colour.
The early morning has a lingering, frosty air — a sharp atmosphere.
All around nature's brush has been busy coating objects with white
     paint.
The pale sunlight breaks through the cloud and mist.
Now the draped silver cobweb glistens with delight as it hangs
     gracefully
Watching the world begin to stir.
Silence — as the warming light flows gently through the brown trees,
Tall and stately — all begin to shed their colourful leaves.
Tossed by the breeze they begin to tumble to the ground
Brown, red, golden — all colours, each one helps
To make a thick, crisp and dry carpet below,
Leaving their home to look like skeletons — cold and bare.

Janet Revell, 15 years

126

Autumn leaf

Leaf of hawthorn, autumn colour,
Droops with loss of chlorophyl,
From a dried and withered stalk,
Sapless veins to curling fingers,
Like a pale hand waving sadly
Its farewell to summer days.

Graham Day, 13 years

127

Autumn

Red berries swaying
yellow leaves fluttering
red apples bouncing on
the road

Valerie Teasdale, 6 years

128

Tree in autumn

There it stands, shivering with its golden life falling to the ground,
making little pit-a-pat noises.

Diane Jackson, 7 years

129

Harvest hymn

How many months does it take to grow
the corn that is reaped in the sun?
And how many months must it rain and shine
before the farmer is done?
How much work and time must it take
before it is ready to bake?
>   The answer my friend is blowin' in the wind
>   The answer is blowin' in the wind.

How many people will be starving this year
of every colour and race?
And how many people will lie on the streets
ashamed to show their face?
And how many people will be hungry this year
before we consider their needs?
>   The answer my friend is blowin' in the wind
>   The answer is blowin' in the wind.

How many people will starve tonight
and how many people will cry?
How much food will be wasted away
by my brothers and sisters and I?
Of all the food that is grown on this land
Why do people still have to die?
>   The answer my friend is blowin' in the wind
>   The answer is blowin' in the wind.

>   *Nicola Chandler, 14 years*
>   *and Teresa Wood, 14 years*

130

Harvest

A wicker basket on a three-legged stool
Full with rosy apples from the tree
A basket full of juicy blackberries
Picked on the rambling common.

Sheaves of corn in a dappled sunlit field
Elderberries hanging in clusters
While above them hang the scarlet berries
Of the towering mountain ash.

A bush of old man's beard tangling
Its fluff-laden wispy stalks together
Under the hips and haws.

For these we thank the Lord.

Janette Watt, 11 years

131

Harvest

Harvest

Golden rich

Summer is ending

Neatly baled in squares

Autumn

Christopher McDonald

132

Winter

Dead, dead-dry, bent-grass joints
sweatless and shrunk with victory
over the curved blue ribs of
past bone-frozen years.
Winter
drips hate raggedly into the unfathomable sky.
Rustling hands quiver over
strong green springing and opening
tight poppy-crimson newborn wetness and
honeysuckle running golden-yellow like bees
of amber carved by the
aeon-long Daedalus-fingered sea.

Georgina Lloyd, 17 years

133

Winter

It was winter.
Barren,
Desolate.
Like an ignored corner
In creation.
Wet earth.
Pools of soiled water:
Raincoats.
Damp leather and
Saturated cloth smelling.
Tree skeletons:
Animal death.
Freak light and
Dark evenings.
Gloom.

It was winter.

John Perry, 13 years

134

Weather

Dear God,
    Our Father,
    Thank you for the weather.

In spring,
    the rain and showers, freshening up the flowers,
    Wakening the sleepy animals. Coming down gently,
    quickly and slowly.
    Thank you for the rain.

In summer,
    the sun and storms, the sun so bright,
    Giving out glory and light, and storms in the night,
    with lightning so frightening,
    and thunder.
    Thank you for these.

In autumn,
    the wind and breezes, blowing through the trees,
    Bringing down their leaves. Sometimes harsh and
    sometimes cool.
    Thank you for the wind.

In winter,
    the snow and fog, crisp and light is the snow.
    It's the trees' scarf, so white. While the fog,
    grey and gloomy,
    sad and sleepy.
    Thank you for these.   Amen

Joanne Dennis, 11 years

135

Christmas

The smell of Christmas in the air,
The smell of turkey everywhere,
Christmas pudding, ever so thick,
There's so much to eat, 'Oh, what shall we pick?'

Trudging through the winter snow,
'Who's that treading on my toe?'
Hardly anyone in the street,
Gone the sound of trudging feet.

Log fires burning ever so bright,
Christmas is here, what a glorious sight!
Wrapping paper, tinsel foil too,
Picking and choosing, 'Oh, how are you?'

Fairy lights make the windows so bright,
And the carol singers, in the night,
So then this is Christmas, I hope it will last,
And I won't think tomorrow it's all in the past.

Caroline Astley, 11 years

136

A longing to share
this light
Devours me
Filling me with
an acute
Awareness
of the enormous
Responsibility
I bear,
too huge to contemplate
Alone,
but rendered
possible
by the Certainty
and Inspiration
of Infinite
Love
manifested in the life
of Jesus Christ.

Mary Wakelin, 18 years

137

The wonderful night

The moon was glowing softly
I hummed a little tune
I sat upon a crumpled rock
Hungry silent and cold
We huddled together like children
Trying to keep warm
The sheep baaing softly
I looked up to the gloomy sky
And saw a strange light
Getting closer and closer
I put my hands above my head so
as it would not blind me
I knocked against the others we were
all scared
What could it be?
Angels were singing so beautiful and
said
Go to Bethlehem where a blessed Baby lies
We took a lamb each
We had nothing else to give
We crept in quietly so as not to disturb him
But he was awake and giggling so sweetly
Mary had wrapped him in swaddling.

Fiona Bonnar, 8 years

138

Birth of a King

Did you see Mary counting the cobwebs
On the stable walls, waiting,
In her fullness, for the time
When she would cry out
Among the straw bales while the
Cattle watched her labour?
That was the birth of a king
That I watch through the glittering
Of a star on my carol sheet.
Did you see the shepherds as they
Stumbled from the snow on the hills
With numb fingers and the filth
Of old sheep under their nails?
Did you see the crown fall
From the head of a king
As he wandered from the warmth
Of his palace into an ice-sodden world
Waiting for summer? There they stand
With their boxes and pout for the Christmas cards.
I wonder how many times they had to
Stop because they had lost the star?

Kaye Tompkins, 17 years

139

Christmas

 Match-stick legs and belly blown,
clutching a bowl of charity rice
in a refugee camp
   Far from home.

 Tired and poor, chilled to the bone
grasping the chance of a stable
Jesus is born
   Far from home.

 Tired from laughter, food and drink
Parcel wrappings litter the floor
Too much on the table
   Is this home?

Mary Wakelin, 13 years

140

Jesus and the crowds

Bodies pushing, shoving, shouting
Always moving, closing in.
Sweating, jostling, restless people
Clamouring to speak with him.

Even crowds at last go homeward
Having taken all they can
And the Giver seeks in silence
Power to be the Son of Man.

Pushing restless men and women
Conveyor belts that never cease
In our world of strife and pressure
We can stop and find his peace.

Mary Wakelin, 14 years

141

Prayer dance

Perfection
Was the child of thought
In a blue robe.
This was the wedding of movement and spirit
A reverence for her beloved.

She dances
As a stream flows clear,
Into an ecstasy of whirlpool.

Softly, arms caress light,
Light feet hold the marble pavement.

She sways, as by breeze,
To the soft inclination of the harp —

And yet she kneels heavily
As if the weight of wood and nails
Was thrown to her delicacy.

This is her way of praying:
A realisation
That His body was broken
While hers remained whole.

Catherine Payne, 15 years

142

Lament for Pilate

Born to witness
A hideous destruction
Sandals pacing and biting the paving
A man of lonely pity
Denied even Judas' strength
Tears of Mary stain his hands like wounds
Standing
Watching the Son sink behind the horizon
Light in the olive groves and gardens
Dimming and fading
Where night spreads like a disease
Greedily swallowing shadows
Intolerance and Rome
Bend and bare his neck, expecting punishment
And wind breathes the echo of his horror
Into skies
Pillars of a city lost
Filling his cold body with penitence
As a ritual accomplished
Denying his innocence.

Catherine Payne, 16 years

143

The owls

No owls watched at Golgotha
in the midnight afternoon
when Christ was carrion
and later when new Roman altars ran
with passive blood — no owls came.

Only when the tiny lights
moved on Iona and Lindisfarne;
when clay shrines smashed:
strong, straight men bowed their heads
in hope of God who did not ask for blood
and women wept at the foot of sterner stones:
when in narrow, chilly cells
pale pens boiled in gold
— then the wide-winged winter owl
tore into the wind
taloned the rising prayers
and screamed the salt night bare as bones.

Oh, our northern gods in exile wait,
patient in unholy, naked trees,
eyeing the silent churchyard,
the priest stooping to his bed
and wait for sacrifice and stained revenge,
when our old blood, clotted with prayers
leaps in the throat with hollow moans
and the owl rushes, vastly still,
poising the knife of the moon,
then tremble
— our great gods return.

Jan Walker, 17 years

144

Nail

Nail
Cool, steel, nail,
Hands
Soft, warm hands,
Nail
Cool, steel, nail,
Feet
Soft, warm feet
On the wooden cross,
His body pinned.
Drugged wine offered,
Refused.
Darkness,
Silence,
Noon to three.
No natural darkness
No normal eclipse.

'My God, my God, why hast thou
    forsaken me?'
The wooden cross pieces silhouetted,
Against the dark sky.
Pain and agony,
Inflicted by nails.
'Let us see if Elijah will save him now,'
The scorning watchers shout.
'Father, forgive them, they know not
    what they do.'
He bowed his head
Hair damp with sweat,
And died.
Nails,
Cool, steel nails,
Limbs,
Cold, hard limbs.

John L. Truelove, 16 years

145

Mortals' immortality

Although mortally wounded,
I live on.
My wound bleeds more blood
As my volume deteriorates.
And with this decrease in size,
My feelings grow in intensity
My belief is never swayed,
Has sometimes faltered.
I have been punched and
    stabbed,
Mutilated, mocked and almost
    murdered,
Yet I continue to live.

And, I shall continue to live
Until time is ended, and
Humanity saved or damned.
My volume will continue to
    deteriorate,
My feelings will continue to
    grow,
My belief will be irresistibly
    strengthened.
You can condemn me,
But never completely kill me —
I was not born to die,
I am Christianity.

David Cahill, 16 years

146

Resurrection morn

A sleepy mist beshrouds the town,
And in the shaded street,
Three stealthy figures move along,
Alert for a retreat.

Their arms are coiled round precious goods
Whose perfume fills the air,
Their voices echo, questioning,
And stammering with fear.

'We'll never move it, it's so big,
And we're not strong enough
It took four men to move the stone,
It's heavy, round and rough.'

At last they reach their promised goal,
Their faces reveal shock.
A gaping chasm lies in front,
'Someone's removed the rock!'

A piercing terror fills their hearts.
They know their Lord has gone,
But somehow they are calmed, until
They venture in the tomb.

The grave clothes lay there undisturbed,
But they feel reassured.
They realise with bubbling joy,
Death could not hold their Lord.

They rush straight out to tell the world,
His friends must quickly know.
'The Lord is risen, he is not dead,
He'll never leave us now.'

Maurita Horsler, 20 years

147

Once upon the crumbling roof

Once upon the crumbling roof
Of a windy church
A song-bird choked in the smoky air,
And all the world below
Died.

No one came to help him,
They thought there was nothing they could do.
So they did nothing.

Until at last a familiar stranger,
(Whom many thought they, perhaps, had seen before)
Arrived.
Alone he revived the creature
With just one warm whispering breath.

Many said, and believed,
There never had been any death
And flung away his truth and, smiling, sighed,
But the chattering song-bird was heard still singing,
Long after these doubters had, smiling, died.

John Jackson, 18 years

148

You know the way I feel

When I masked my true feelings with pretences of contentment,
You gazed through my disguise,
Uncovered all my faults and lies,
And saw me as I was.
You saw the chasm deep and black,
You saw the pain, the love I lacked,
The shadows of my guilt:
You knew the way I felt.

Soon, in a state of painful thought, I fell inside my soul.
Its murky air felt dank and cold;
My feet were lost in frosty mist
And the chill wind blew,
Scattering damp and muddy leaves,
Unseen, into my face.
Terrified, I trembled,
Sweating long into the humid night,
Till tears and perspiration stood collecting at my feet —
A pool, a lake, a sea
In which I wished to drown,
Until your sun began to rise.
Your light shone out across the waters,
Kindling bright fires inside my soul.
It burned with loving thrill.
I was calm, I'm happy still:
You know the way I feel!

Derek Walker, 17 years

149

The day of Pentecost

The path of destruction
Is all one can see
Of the riotous wind.
It rips houses
From their foundations
And plucks trees
From the ground.
It makes families homeless.
This is
Devastation.
Then there is the gentle breeze
Cooling the hot brow
In summer.
Gently rustling the green leaves.
But no wind was
So gentle
And yet
So mighty
As the coming of the Holy Spirit.

Jenny Mabbott, 14 years

150

Violence

The Romans and the early Christians ...
Fought what seemed an endless war.
How different were their methods.
The Christian's arrows were his words ...
His sword was his great faith.
His arenas were the meetings held in darkened rooms or on green
    hills.
The Romans found out to their cost
That these weapons were more than enough
To combat their own of steel, torture, and the Coliseum.
Here the lions roared and leapt on the defenceless heads
That were bowed in prayer or defiantly lifted to the sky,
Singing praises to their God on high.

When it is asked, 'Who won this war?'
'Tis here for all to see,
A list of Martyrs, Saints — gentle folk,
Who died for you and me.

Helen Finney, 11 years

151

What we need, not what we want

In this world of war and strife,
The bomb, the gun, the gas, the knife,
The dangling rope, the hangman's grin,
All of us are black with sin.
Do you feel a need for God,
The one and only sturdy rod,
The rod on which I rest all day
To guide me in the rightful way?
This way leads to eternal life
With no more sin or war or strife.

Gregory Wilde, 13 years

152

God?

Who is God?
	What is God?
Is he really true?
	Does he work wonders?
I wish I knew.

Is he in the green trees?
	Is he in the meadow?
Is he in the latest beat?
	Is he in the twisting feet?
Is he real?
	Is he true?
Oh! I say! I wish I knew!
			J. Fairbairn, 13 years

153

This I ask you, God

Who is God?
What is God?
These are the questions I ask you, Lord.
Why must I breathe to live?
Why must I eat to stay alive?
These are the questions I ask you, Lord.

Why have you let people starve to death?
Have they done you any wrong?
Why do I get ill?
Do I do you ill?

Who are you, God?
Did you really create mankind?
Why must all these things happen?
This I ask you, God.
			Barry Kriefman, 12 years

154

Where was God?

And where was God
When war broke out?
Where was he, not to hear them shout?
Where was God when aloud they cried?
Where was God when they died?
Where was God when blood was spilt?
Was he asleep
Or was he aware
Or was he fighting the devil?

D. Williamson

155

A modern psalm

The Lord creates me, in him will I trust.
Through times good or bad I will follow him,
Ready to be shown the wonders he sets before me.
As he is the Shepherd, so I am the lamb.

No supermarket can work like this —
He asks nothing in return; though he wants me to love him.
I must not delay; the choice is there for the taking
But I must decide.

Anon

156

Life's balance

There is no balance to life without God.
God is like the gyrostabiliser in a gyroscope.
God is stability.
Without him there is no meaning to life.
Things would be upset.
God is nature.
There is a satisfaction in knowing that God is in all the modern
   machinery, in nuclear components and electricity.
There is satisfaction in the knowledge that we have someone to
   depend on, although we ourselves must run our lives.
God is strength.
God is the inventor, the Father, and we are his fast learning children.
God is learning.
God is within all music; he is a conductor who conducts the system of
   life and nature in his music.
God composes life.
The composition could not be possible without an original blueprint.
God is the draughtsman.
God does not help all of the needy and those in distress for he wishes
   men to help each other, bringing them closer together, no matter
   what the colour of their skin.
God encourages love.

Paul Tappenden, 14 years

157

I am not afraid

The sun has disappeared.
I have switched off the light,
and my wife and children are asleep.
The animals in the forest are full of fear,
and so are the people on their mats.
They prefer the day with your sun
to the night.
But I still know that
your moon is there,
and your eyes
and also your hands.
Thus I am not afraid.
This day again
you led us wonderfully.
Everybody went to his mat
satisfied and full.
Renew us during our sleep,
that in the morning
we may come afresh to our daily jobs.
Be with our brothers far away in Asia
who may be getting up now.
Amen

A young Ghanaian

158

No God and proud of it

Under the hammer and sickle lie my views.
Be gone, wretched pulpit, priest and pew!
God is the state
And factory capacity; not Heaven my bait.

Yet dally awhile and ponder deep,
For now you're a vegetable, waiting to be reaped.
Gone is your protection and guidance from above.

Gone is the creator's fatherly love.
Death means the end now for you,
And no eternity is yours to woo.

Still, should I believe these Jewish Tales,
Of God and Mercy, and Galilean Gales?
Forward, let us march right on
To a Soviet Society with proud aplomb.
There will be factories, houses and
Offices to the sky, and — and —
In the end, just dust and sand.
Give me back my God.

Roy Smith, 15 years

A matter of life and death

159

Death

Who knows the secrets of death?
An exit or an entrance?
The flesh disappears:
The memory lingers on,
Until that too
Falls into oblivion's bottomless pit.

Death:
The front door of heavenly paradise?
The golden gates of eternal utopia?
Or is it a final
Existence-ceasing
End?

John Perry, 13 years

160

Full circle

Your joy had gone;
Your love had spent his time.
Untimely Death had played his part,
His lines were said;
The book of life was
Finished,
Ended.
Good times, bad times,
Rich and poor;
But Death had parted you,
The door between was shut.
Brave thoughts, brave words.
You vowed never to love again;
You said that
Faith and mourning was your part;
And yet inside,
Doubt,
Fear tore your mind,
Despair of life and
Suicide was in your brain.

That night memories filled your head,
They drowned your thought;
Tears wet your cheeks;
The sweetness of recollection
Was bitter in your mouth;
His gentle face,
A knife ripped your soul.
And when the struggle with the
Past was at its end,
Sleep came upon you,
Peace that resolved your fate.

When you woke,
The newly risen sun
Kissed your frosted window.
Strength had returned.
You had the will to live your life,
The courage to be free.
The wheel of time had turned full circle;
And from the ashes of his Death
Was born new Life.

Roger Dunn, 17 years

161

Sitting alone by a cold gas fire,
So cold, unable to feel cold any more.
A summer, a young girl
In Victorian dress, running wildly
Through the field.
The cold, the cold, so cold,
Penetrating through the bones,
A child standing alone in a schoolroom,
Standing in the corner, alone, waiting,
An old woman sitting alone, waiting.
A child in an exam room,
Busily writing, then pausing, thinking,
Writing again in continuing circle.
A child in a playroom,
Alone, with only dolls for company,
Changing to a young woman, alone in an office
An old woman, a young child,
A young woman waiting.

Now the waiting is over,
'Such a shame, a sweet old dear.'
'Poor old soul, three days dead they say.'
A coffin in a hearse,
No flowers, no mourners,
Alone,
All three are dead.

R.D., 17 years

162

Time (Prologue)

Time —
We can see it in the waving of the meadow grass;
    Time —
We can hear it in the ticking of the pendulum;
       Time —
We can feel it in the wind of change still blowing by;
         Time walks slowly on.

Time —
It lay dormant in the realms of pre-eternity;
    Time —
In the hour of Satan's lust for Pride it was conceived;
      Time —
It still scars the forehead of a man with lines of age;
      Time leads men to grief.

Time —
It is mitigation for the acts of wicked men;
    Time —
Oh, the old excuse! When will men ever see its lie?
      Time —
They will be judged by a God who has pierced through its shell;
      Time calls, 'Soon to die!'

Derek Walker, 17 years

163

To you who were left behind

For you who loved, time was Eternity
  While you stood still, the world
                          Went on,
You lived and loved and life
                   Was gold,
  But now your days are long
                   And love is gone,
You find the world's still young
  And you are old.
And so exhausted, empty, grey
  You turn round only
To see Love run the other way
  And leave you lonely.
'Time was, and is, (and now that
Life's no more) shall be ...
              ... Eternity.'

Joanne Batch, 16 years

164

Who cares?

The cold grey dawn arrives,
Scattering
Half-hearted rays
Over the black roof tops,
Another day.

What am I living for?
Nobody
Visits me.
What do people care?
Nothing.

Why should they care?
Grandfather clock
Ticking endlessly;
Time has no meaning
Now.

The cold bites my body,
Numbing
My very soul,
What have I done to deserve
Loneliness?

Why should I live?
My heart
Sobs within me.
I think I'll just lie here and
Die.

As dusk kisses the dark chimneys,
A stiff
Body lies in a slum.
Who cares?
Nobody.

Headlines — three weeks later.
Death.
Old lady dies in slum;
Neighbours found her
Yesterday.

Sharon Clough, 14 years

165

It is not good

It is not good
To watch an old man die;
A high domed forehead, fringed with silver silk,
Transparent ivory ears,
That hear no more,
A sharp beaked nose, networked with thin red skeins
Above a drooped moustache,
And bloodless lips, brown scummed,
Mumbling to long dead friends,
While scrawny throat
Flutters like captive bird
And alabaster fingers, nails too clean,
Fumble the starched sheet.

Around the ward, each in his captive bed,
Lie waxwork figures, graven, listless, mute,
White haired and open mouthed,
Blank-eyed and still.
By each bedside table, water glass,
An orange or an apple,
Grapes or flowers,
Gifts from the living to the dying dead.

On stools by each the watching relatives,
A yard away but separate
By gulf unbridgeable,
Sit in a world of sterile cleanness,
Groping for words to speak,
The world of life confronting world of death.

Outside the streets are wet,
The traffic roars;
The living hurry by, intent on life,
Unmindful of the room
Where old men lie
Awaiting death.
It is not good to watch an old man die.

                              S. Clafton, 14 years

166

The tree

The tree is stripped bare now
It shudders slightly;
A cold wind sweeps it clean
Grey sky relieves each perfect twig
— The house behind looks so innocent
What has it known of this?

Each branch moves from the trunk
Its own special mystery
Its roots reach deep down:
Submerged; yet strong.
How deep are your foundations, house?

Spring will come; one day
Decking you in gay attire
— And Summer too, full promise of new life,
Will come; then Autumn's golden warmth
Returns.

Yet are you not at your best now,
Stark and beautiful?
You hide not behind images;
Reach not for What You May Not Have.

Why fret when such as this is here?
But now a rattle shakes your frame
The saw cuts deep
You sway more now, past years of life
From seed to fruit
Flash by.
And with a crash you fall:
I ask you
— Why?

Anon

167

Rain

Soon
I will be dead.
Falling
At terrific speed
Around me:
My companions:
Some already dead:
Blots on the earth.

The landscape
Ascending towards me.
At first:
The jump.
Panic and confusion.
But now
Absolute terror.

I am going to die.
I
Am going to die.
But
No. No!
Oh God!
I don't want to die.

My life:
Only a minute's length.

The cloud
Expelling its prisoners:
Throwing them to the ground
In a sadistic massacre.
Oh God!
I don't want ...

                    John Perry, 12 years

168

The old priest

The whitewashed walls are peeling,
And the stone is showing through,
There are cobwebs on the ceiling,
And bats in the belfry too.
The old brown pews are beyond repair,
The hymn books are worn and old,
The old black priest with whiting hair
Is shivering in the cold.
He carries out his service
As though the folk were there,
But the whitewashed walls are peeling
And in each book, a tear.
He's old and very weary
And he can hardly see
But he says the time's gone quickly
For everyone but he.

Bridget Rawlence, 11 years

169

Memory

The vicar slowly climbs the pulpit stair.
His wife sits fumbling in the organ loft.
No congregation, 'What's the point?' they say.
Even the grave-digger has gone away.
As he begins his solitary sermon
He stops, remembering some other days.
He was a student, full of new ideas.
Here was his mission. He would save the world.
Now who is saved? He cannot even tell.
The newspaper is always three days late.
It was not he who saved them. That he knows.
Rotting away, with ivied monuments.
There sits his wife, wrapped in a tartan rug.
Playing 'Jerusalem' to please the mice.
'What life is this?' he thinks. But numbed by years
His brain does not reply, just sleeps again.

Clarissa Browne, 14 years

170

An old man

The village was as quiet as
the death of the headman.

The wind was blowing smoothly against the sea shore
        and the shaded trees
        where there was nobody
        but an old man, whose peers have died long ago.

The old man sat for a while thinking
        about the old and the new.

And said, where are my people?
Where are they now?
        These were the major thoughts
        that appeared in his mind.
        Then, there was a cracking sound
        that disturbed the old man.
What was it? A man? A child?
No, it was a falling house.

The house that was built long ago.
Again Taulai, the old man, thought of the owner
and the owners of the old canoes
behind the rotten platforms
everything is old and rotten,
nobody caring for them.

They are away, in towns,
in schools, in new stations.
Taulai bent his head and
found himself crying aloud.

                        Anon, Papua New Guinea

171

I remember

I remember, I remember,
My old haunted house
And the garden had not a blade of grass
And all the cupboards were mouldy:
In my room it's pitch dark at night.

I remember, I remember,
The bare trees of winter
And the sweet smelling flowers in Spring:
In winter the snow and frost would chock them,
And in Autumn the leaves would turn brown.

I remember, I remember,
Down the old cellar
Where it was dirty and horrible:
And where a dim oil lamp was placed on the shelf,
Was only put out at night.
I feel sad for the old house
Guess why!
Because it is going to be demolished.

Sharon Miles, 12 years

ACKNOWLEDGEMENTS

Every effort has been made to trace the authors of the material in this anthology and to obtain copyright permissions. Apologies are offered to any whose work has been used but not suitably acknowledged owing to lack of information and any such errors will be corrected in subsequent editions.

The compiler is grateful to the following publishers, associations and compilers who have allowed their previously published and copyright material to be reproduced in this anthology.

The City of Birmingham Education Department from *Images of Youth* (Items 26, 28, 57-58, 61, 89, 92, 115, 120, 171)

The Headmistress, Blyth Jex School, Norwich from *Writings 1975* (Items 40, 74, 87, 90, 96, 106, 117, 161)

The Headmaster, Breckenborough School, Thirsk (Item 154)

The County of Cambridge Education Department from *At the Rainbow's Foot* (Items 20, 125-126, 144)

Chatto & Windus (Educational)/Granada Publishing Ltd from *The Excitement of Writing* by the County Council of the West Riding of Yorkshire (Item 38)

The Church Missionary Society from *Morning, Noon and Night* (Items 5, 157)

The Headmaster, Clifton College, Bristol from *Clifton College Writing, Spring 1969* (Item 19)

The Council for World Mission from *Hisopang* magazine of Gaulim Training College, Papua New Guinea (Item 170)

Cumbria County Council Education Department from *Finding the Words* (Items 2, 9, 24, 32, 43, 53, 69-70, 73, 99, 107, 116, 127-128, 131, 137, 143, 165) and from *Seize on Life* (Items 15, 21, 44-45, 48, 50, 54-55, 145)

The Headmaster, Eaton (City of Norwich) School (Items 14, 91, 113, 119, 147, 151, 160, 164)

The Headmaster, Ecclesfield Comprehensive School from *The Ecclesfieldian,* the magazine of the former Ecclesfield Grammar School (Item 22)

Mr Geoffrey Hacker, joint compiler of *Conflict 1* (Items 25, 42, copyright of which is held by the authors)

Mr Raymond Hearn, compiler of *Modern Psalms by Boys* (Items 109-110, 152-153, 156, 158)

The Warden, Impington Village College, Cambridge (Item 52)

3M Young Poet Awards Scheme (Items 16, 29, 138, 141-142)

The Methodist Church Overseas Division from *Window 1976* (Items 3, 111, 134)

The National Association for the Teaching of English: the Bristol Association (Item 76) and the S W Lancs and Merseyside Branch from *Poems from Primary Schools* (Items 7-8, 34, 59)

The National Christian Education Council from *Search for Meaning* by Irene Champernowne (Item 49)

The National Society for Mentally Handicapped Children from *Answer Me World* (Items 81-84, 86)

The Headmistress, Norwich High School (G P D S T) (Items 4, 23, 35-36, 47, 68, 93, 95, 97-98, 103, 121, 124, 132, 163, 168-169)

The Poetry Society, organisers of the Poets in School project; to Book Club Associates, who designed, produced and published the selection *Poets in School* for their members; and to George Harrap & Company, who publish the general edition (Items 10, 27, 46, 62, 94)

The Headmaster, Priory Junior School, Tynemouth (Items 18, 102, 118)

Speedwell Comprehensive School, Bristol from *Helix 1973* (Items 60, 75, 88, 114, 166)

The compiler is grateful to the following children and young people who have allowed their previously unpublished work to be included in this anthology. They retain the copyright of their own items and permission to reproduce them should be made to the compiler.

Fleur Anderson (Items 100-101)
Caroline Astley (Items 77, 135)
Stephen Bateman (Item 39)
Nicola Chandler (Item 129)
Claire Dorer (Item 33)
Helen Finney (Item 150)
Nigel Forman (Item 72)
David Hazeldine (Item 112)
Maurita Horsler (Item 146)
Jean Killett (Items 63-66, 104)
Judith Leon (Item 71)
Jenny Mabbott (Item 149)
John Perry (Items 11-13, 37, 67, 105, 122, 133, 159, 167)
Julie Rains (Items 17, 123)
Alan Rodgers (Item 80)
Stuart Scott (Items 31, 85)
Pam Sephton (Item 41)
Mary Wakelin (Items 1, 6, 30, 136, 139, 140)
Derek Walker (Items 148, 162)
Janette Watt (Item 130)
Teresa Wood (Item 129)

INDEX

The index has been designed to guide readers to items covering subjects and themes which are frequently used in Christian worship and religious education in day schools and churches.

The numbers in italics indicate whole sections.